PRAISE FOR RICHARD P. FEYNMAN AND

"What Do <u>You</u> Care What Other People Think?"

"There is nothing obtuse or difficult about [this] book. Indeed, Feynman's rendering of such a potentially complex subject as the *Challenger* disaster is straightforward, lucid, and accessible."
—*San Francisco Chronicle*

"One of the greatest minds of the twentieth century. . . . [He] was also stubborn, irreverent, playful, intensely curious and highly original in practically everything he did."
—*New York Review of Books*

"A gentler book [than *"Surely You're Joking, Mr. Feynman!"*], and for those interested in the man, a more substantial one."
—Bettyann Kevles, *Los Angeles Times*

"Exceptional."
—*Minneapolis Star Tribune*

"Extremely readable and enjoyable."
—Natasha Samani, *Medium*

"Brings Feynman to life in all his wonderful and multiple dimensions. Marvelous."
—*Kirkus Reviews*

"The book's second half is the high point; it is topical, entertaining, and illuminating, and tells of Feynman's work on the Rogers Commission, which investigated the *Challenger* space shuttle disaster."
—*Library Journal*

" '*What Do <u>You</u> Care What Other People Think?*' touches genuine depths of feeling. . . . Feynman displays . . . the adventurousness that captivated readers of '*Surely You're Joking, Mr. Feynman!*'"
—*Publishers Weekly*

OTHER WORKS BY RICHARD P. FEYNMAN

Classic Feynman

No Ordinary Genius

"Surely You're Joking, Mr. Feynman!"

"What Do <u>You</u> Care What Other People Think?"

FURTHER
ADVENTURES OF A
CURIOUS CHARACTER

RICHARD P. FEYNMAN
AS TOLD TO RALPH LEIGHTON

W. W. Norton & Company
Independent Publishers Since 1923
New York · London

For information about permission to reproduce selections from this book,
write to Permissions, W. W. Norton & Company, Inc.,
500 Fifth Avenue, New York, NY 10110

For information about special discounts for bulk purchases, please contact
W. W. Norton Special Sales at specialsales@wwnorton.com or 800-233-4830

Manufacturing by LSC Communications Harrisonburg, VA
Book design by Chris Welch
Production manager: Andrea Grant

Library of Congress Cataloging-in-Publication Data
Feynman, Richard Phillips.
"What do you care what other people think?" : further adventures of
a curious character/by Richard P. Feynman, as told to Ralph
Leighton
p. cm.
Includes index.
1. Feynman, Richard Phillips. 2. Physicists—United States—
Biography. 3. Science—Anecdotes. I. Leighton, Ralph.
II. Title.
QC16.F49A3 1988
530'.9'2'—dc19
[B]

ISBN 978-0-393-35564-2 pbk.

W. W. Norton & Company, Inc.
500 Fifth Avenue, New York, N.Y. 10110
www.wwnorton.com

W. W. Norton & Company Ltd.
15 Carlisle Street, London W1D 3BS

1 2 3 4 5 6 7 8 9 0

Contents

Part 2
MR. FEYNMAN GOES TO WASHINGTON: INVESTIGATING THE SPACE SHUTTLE *CHALLENGER* DISASTER

EPILOGUE

Preface

Because of the appearance of *"Surely You're Joking, Mr. Feynman!"* a few things need to be explained here.

First, although the central character in this book is the same as before, the "adventures of a curious character" here are different: some are light and some tragic, but most of the time Mr. Feynman is surely *not* joking—although it's often hard to tell.

Second, the stories in this book fit together more loosely than those in *"Surely You're Joking . . . ,"* where they were arranged chronologically to give a semblance of order. (That resulted in some readers getting the mistaken idea that *SYJ* is an autobiography.) My motivation is simple: ever since hearing my first Feynman stories, I have had the powerful desire to share them with others.

Finally, most of these stories were not told at drumming sessions, as before. I will elaborate on this in the brief outline that follows.

Part 1, "A Curious Character," begins by describing the influence of those who most shaped Feynman's personality—

his father, Mel, and his first love, Arlene. The first story was adapted from "The Pleasure of Finding Things Out," a BBC program produced by Christopher Sykes. The story of Arlene, from which the title of this book was taken, was painful for Feynman to recount. It was assembled over the past ten years out of pieces from six different stories. When it was finally complete, Feynman was especially fond of this story, and happy to share it with others.

The other Feynman stories in Part 1, although generally lighter in tone, are included here because there won't be a second volume of *SYJ*. Feynman was particularly proud of "It's as Simple as One, Two, Three . . . ," which he occasionally thought of writing up as a psychology paper. The letters in the last chapter of Part 1 have been provided courtesy of Gweneth Feynman, Freeman Dyson, and Henry Bethe.

Part 2, "Mr. Feynman Goes to Washington," is, unfortunately, Feynman's last big adventure. The story is particularly long because its content is still timely. (Shorter versions have appeared in *Engineering and Science* and *Physics Today*.) It was not published sooner because Feynman underwent his third and fourth major surgeries—plus radiation, hyperthermia, and other treatments—since serving on the Rogers Commission.

Feynman's decade-long battle against cancer ended on February 15, 1988, two weeks after he taught his last class at Caltech. I decided to include one of his most eloquent and inspirational speeches, "The Value of Science," as an epilogue.

Ralph Leighton
March 1988

PART 1

A Curious Character

THE MAKING OF A SCIENTIST

I have a friend who's an artist, and he sometimes takes a view which I don't agree with. He'll hold up a flower and say, "Look how beautiful it is," and I'll agree. But then he'll say, "I, as an artist, can see how beautiful a flower is. But you, as a scientist, take it all apart and it becomes dull." I think he's kind of nutty.

First of all, the beauty that he sees is available to other people—and to me, too, I believe. Although I might not be quite as refined aesthetically as he is, I can appreciate the beauty of a flower. But at the same time, I see much more in the flower than he sees. I can imagine the cells inside, which also have a beauty. There's beauty not just at the dimension of one centimeter; there's also beauty at a smaller dimension.

There are the complicated actions of the cells, and other processes. The fact that the colors in the flower have evolved in order to attract insects to pollinate it is interesting; that means insects can see the colors. That adds a question: does this aesthetic sense we have also exist in lower forms of life? There are all kinds of interesting questions that come from a knowledge of science, which only adds to the excitement and mystery and awe of a flower. It only adds. I don't understand how it subtracts.

I've always been very one-sided about science, and when I was younger I concentrated almost all my effort on it. In those days I didn't have time, and I didn't have much patience, to learn what's called the humanities. Even though there were humanities courses in the university that you had to take in order to graduate, I tried my best to avoid them. It's only afterwards, when I've gotten older and more relaxed, that I've spread out a little bit. I've learned to draw and I read a little bit, but I'm really still a very one-sided person and I don't know a great deal. I have a limited intelligence and I use it in a particular direction.

Before I was born, my father told my mother, "If it's a boy, he's going to be a scientist."* When I was just a little kid, very small in a highchair, my father brought home a lot of little bathroom tiles—seconds—of different colors. We played with them, my father setting them up vertically on my highchair like dominoes, and I would push one end so they would all go down.

Then after a while, I'd help set them up. Pretty soon, we're setting them up in a more complicated way: two white tiles and a blue tile, two white tiles and a blue tile, and so on. When my mother saw that she said, "Leave the poor child alone. If he wants to put a blue tile, let him put a blue tile."

---

* Richard's younger sister, Joan, has a Ph.D. in physics, in spite of this preconception that only boys are destined to be scientists.

But my father said, "No, I want to show him what patterns are like and how interesting they are. It's a kind of elementary mathematics." So he started very early to tell me about the world and how interesting it is.

We had the *Encyclopaedia Britannica* at home. When I was a small boy he used to sit me on his lap and read to me from the *Britannica*. We would be reading, say, about dinosaurs. It would be talking about the *Tyrannosaurus rex*, and it would say something like, "This dinosaur is twenty-five feet high and its head is six feet across."

My father would stop reading and say, "Now, let's see what that means. That would mean that if he stood in our front yard, he would be tall enough to put his head through our window up here." (We were on the second floor.) "But his head would be too wide to fit in the window." Everything he read to me he would translate as best he could into some reality.

It was very exciting and very, very interesting to think there were animals of such magnitude—and that they all died out, and that nobody knew why. I wasn't frightened that there would be one coming in my window as a consequence of this. But I learned from my father to translate: everything I read I try to figure out what it really means, what it's really saying.

We used to go to the Catskill Mountains, a place where people from New York City would go in the summer. The fathers would all return to New York to work during the week, and come back only for the weekend. On weekends, my father would take me for walks in the woods and he'd tell me about interesting things that were going on in the woods. When the other mothers saw this, they thought it was wonderful and that the other fathers should take their sons for walks. They tried to work on them but they didn't get anywhere at first.

They wanted my father to take all the kids, but he didn't want to because he had a special relationship with me. So it ended up that the other fathers had to take their children for walks the next weekend.

The next Monday, when the fathers were all back at work, we kids were playing in a field. One kid says to me, "See that bird? What kind of bird is that?"

I said, "I haven't the slightest idea what kind of a bird it is."

He says, "It's a brown-throated thrush. Your father doesn't teach you anything!"

But it was the opposite. He had already taught me: "See that bird?" he says. "It's a Spencer's warbler." (I knew he didn't know the real name.) "Well, in Italian, it's a *Chutto Lapittida*. In Portuguese, it's a *Bom da Peida*. In Chinese, it's a *Chung-long-tah*, and in Japanese, it's a *Katano Tekeda*. You can know the name of that bird in all the languages of the world, but when you're finished, you'll know absolutely nothing whatever about the bird. You'll only know about humans in different places, and what they call the bird. So let's look at the bird and see what it's *doing*—that's what counts." (I learned very early the difference between knowing the name of something and knowing something.)

He said, "For example, look: the bird pecks at its feathers all the time. See it walking around, pecking at its feathers?"

"Yeah."

He says, "Why do you think birds peck at their feathers?"

I said, "Well, maybe they mess up their feathers when they fly, so they're pecking them in order to straighten them out."

"All right," he says. "If that were the case, then they would peck a lot just after they've been flying. Then, after they've been on the ground a while, they wouldn't peck so much any more—you know what I mean?"

"Yeah."

He says, "Let's look and see if they peck more just after they land."

It wasn't hard to tell: there was not much difference between the birds that had been walking around a bit and those that had just landed. So I said, "I give up. Why does a bird peck at its feathers?"

"Because there are lice bothering it," he says. "The lice eat flakes of protein that come off its feathers."

He continued, "Each louse has some waxy stuff on its legs, and little mites eat that. The mites don't digest it perfectly, so they emit from their rear ends a sugar-like material, in which bacteria grow."

Finally he says, "So you see, everywhere there's a source of food, there's *some* form of life that finds it."

Now, I knew that it may not have been exactly a louse, that it might not be exactly true that the louse's legs have mites. That story was probably incorrect in *detail*, but what he was telling me was right in *principle*.

Another time, when I was older, he picked a leaf off of a tree. This leaf had a flaw, a thing we never look at much. The leaf was sort of deteriorated; it had a little brown line in the shape of a C, starting somewhere in the middle of the leaf and going out in a curl to the edge.

"Look at this brown line," he says. "It's narrow at the beginning and it's wider as it goes to the edge. What this is, is a fly—a blue fly with yellow eyes and green wings has come and laid an egg on this leaf. Then, when the egg hatches into a maggot (a caterpillar-like thing), it spends its whole life eating this leaf—that's where it gets its food. As it eats along, it leaves behind this brown trail of eaten leaf. As the maggot grows, the trail grows wider until he's grown to full size at the end of the leaf, where he turns into a fly—a blue fly with yellow eyes and green wings—who flies away and lays an egg on another leaf."

Again, I knew that the details weren't precisely correct—it could have even been a beetle—but the idea that he was trying to explain to me was the amusing part of life: the whole thing is just reproduction. No matter how complicated the business is, the main point is to do it again!

Not having experience with many fathers, I didn't realize how remarkable he was. How did he learn the deep principles of science and the love of it, what's behind it, and why it's worth doing? I never really asked him, because I just assumed that those were things that fathers knew.

My father taught me to notice things. One day, I was playing with an "express wagon," a little wagon with a railing around it. It had a ball in it, and when I pulled the wagon, I noticed something about the way the ball moved. I went to my father and said, "Say, Pop, I noticed something. When I pull the wagon, the ball rolls to the back of the wagon. And when I'm pulling it along and I suddenly stop, the ball rolls to the front of the wagon. Why is that?"

"That, nobody knows," he said. "The general principle is that things which are moving tend to keep on moving, and things which are standing still tend to stand still, unless you push them hard. This tendency is called 'inertia,' but nobody knows why it's true." Now, that's a deep understanding. He didn't just give me the name.

He went on to say, "If you look from the side, you'll see that it's the back of the wagon that you're pulling against the ball, and the ball stands still. As a matter of fact, from the friction it starts to move forward a little bit in relation to the ground. It doesn't move back."

I ran back to the little wagon and set the ball up again and pulled the wagon. Looking sideways, I saw that indeed he was right. Relative to the sidewalk, it moved forward a little bit.

That's the way I was educated by my father, with those kinds of examples and discussions: no pressure—just lovely, interesting discussions. It has motivated me for the rest of my life, and makes me interested in *all* the sciences. (It just happens I do physics better.)

I've been caught, so to speak—like someone who was given something wonderful when he was a child, and he's always looking for it again. I'm always looking, like a child, for the wonders I know I'm going to find—maybe not every time, but every once in a while.

Around that time my cousin, who was three years older, was in high school. He was having considerable difficulty with his algebra, so a tutor would come. I was allowed to sit in a corner while the tutor would try to teach my cousin algebra. I'd hear him talking about x.

I said to my cousin, "What are you trying to do?"

"I'm trying to find out what x is, like in $2x + 7 = 15$."

I say, "You mean 4."

"Yeah, but you did it by arithmetic. You have to do it by algebra."

I learned algebra, fortunately, not by going to school, but by finding my aunt's old schoolbook in the attic, and understanding that the whole idea was to find out what x is—it doesn't make any difference how you do it. For me, there was no such thing as doing it "by arithmetic," or doing it "by algebra." "Doing it by algebra" was a set of rules which, if you followed them blindly, could produce the answer: "subtract 7 from both sides; if you have a multiplier, divide both sides by the multiplier," and so on—a series of steps by which you could get the answer if you didn't understand what you were trying to do. The rules had been invented so that the children who have to study algebra can all pass it. And that's why my cousin was never able to do algebra.

There was a series of math books in our local library which started out with *Arithmetic for the Practical Man*. Then came *Algebra for the Practical Man*, and then *Trigonometry for the Practical Man*. (I learned trigonometry from that, but I soon forgot it again, because I didn't understand it very well.) When I was about thirteen, the library was going to get *Calculus for the Practical Man*. By this time I knew, from reading the encyclopedia, that calculus was an important and interesting subject, and I ought to learn it.

When I finally saw the calculus book at the library, I was very excited. I went to the librarian to check it out, but she looked at me and said, "You're just a child. What are you taking this book out for?"

It was one of the few times in my life I was uncomfortable and I lied. I said it was for my father.

I took the book home and I began to learn calculus from it. I thought it was relatively simple and straightforward. My father started to read it, but he found it confusing and he couldn't understand it. So I tried to explain calculus to him. I didn't know he was so limited, and it bothered me a little bit. It was the first time I realized that I had learned more in some sense than he.

One of the things that my father taught me besides physics—whether it's correct or not—was a disrespect for certain kinds of things. For example, when I was a little boy, and he would sit me on his knee, he'd show me rotogravures in the *New York Times*—that's printed pictures which had just come out in newspapers.

One time we were looking at a picture of the pope and everybody bowing in front of him. My father said, "Now, look at those humans. Here's one human standing here, and all these others are bowing in front of him. Now, what's the difference? This one is the pope"—he hated the pope anyway. He said, "This difference is the hat he's wearing." (If it was a general, it was the epaulets. It was always the costume, the uniform, the position.) "But," he said, "this man has the same problems as everybody else: he eats dinner; he goes to the bathroom. He's a human being." (By the way, my father was in the uniform business, so he knew what the difference is in a man with the uniform off and the uniform on—it was the same man for him.)

He was happy with me, I believe. Once, though, when I came back from MIT (I'd been there a few years), he said to me, "Now that you've become educated about these things, there's one question I've always had that I've never understood very well."

I asked him what it was.

He said, "I understand that when an atom makes a transition from one state to another, it emits a particle of light called a photon."

"That's right," I said.

He says, "Is the photon in the atom ahead of time?"

"No, there's no photon beforehand."

"Well," he says, "where does it come from, then? How does it come out?"

I tried to explain it to him—that photon numbers aren't conserved; they're just created by the motion of the electron—but I couldn't explain it very well. I said, "It's like the sound that I'm making now: it wasn't in me before." (It's not like my little boy, who suddenly announced one day, when he was very young, that he could no longer say a certain word—the word turned out to be "cat"—because his "word bag" had run out of the word. There's no word bag that makes you use up words as they come out; in the same sense, there's no "photon bag" in an atom.)

He was not satisfied with me in that respect. I was never able to explain any of the things that he didn't understand. So he was unsuccessful: he sent me to all these universities in order to find out those things, and he never did find out.

Although my mother didn't know anything about science, she had a great influence on me as well. In particular, she had a wonderful sense of humor, and I learned from her that the highest forms of understanding we can achieve are laughter and human compassion.

"WHAT DO <u>YOU</u> CARE WHAT OTHER PEOPLE THINK?"

When I was a young fella, about thirteen, I had somehow gotten in with a group of guys who were a little older than I was, and more sophisticated. They knew a lot of different girls, and would go out with them—often to the beach.

One time when we were at the beach, most of the guys had gone out on some jetty with the girls. I was interested in a particular girl a little bit, and sort of thought out loud: "Gee, I think I'd like to take Barbara to the movies . . ."

That's all I had to say, and the guy next to me gets all excited. He runs out onto the rocks and finds her. He pushes her back, all the while saying in a loud voice, "Feynman has something he wants to say to you, Barbara!" It was most embarrassing.

Pretty soon the guys are all standing around me, saying, "Well, *say* it, Feynman!" So I invited her to the movies. It was my first date.

I went home and told my mother about it. She gave me all kinds of advice on how to do this and that. For example, if we take the bus, I'm supposed to get off the bus first, and offer Barbara my hand. Or if we have to walk in the street, I'm supposed to walk on the outside. She even told me what kinds of things to say. She was handing down a cultural tradition to me: the women teach their sons how to treat the next generation of women well.

After dinner, I get all slicked up and go to Barbara's house to call for her. I'm nervous. She isn't ready, of course (it's always like that), so her family has me wait for her in the dining room, where they're eating with friends—a lot of people. They say things like, "Isn't he cute!" and all kinds of other stuff. I didn't feel cute. It was absolutely terrible!

I remember everything about the date. As we walked from her house to the new, little theater in town, we talked about playing the piano. I told her how, when I was younger, they made me learn piano for a while, but after six months I was still playing "Dance of the Daisies," and couldn't stand it any more. You see, I was worried about being a sissy, and to be stuck for weeks playing "Dance of the Daisies" was too much for me, so I quit. I was so sensitive about being a sissy that it even bothered me when my mother sent me to the market to buy some snacks called Peppermint Patties and Toasted Dainties.

We saw the movie, and I walked her back to her home. I complimented her on the nice, pretty gloves she was wearing. Then I said goodnight to her on the doorstep.

Barbara says to me, "Thank you for a very lovely evening."

"You're welcome!" I answered. I felt terrific.

The next time I went out on a date—it was with a different girl—I say goodnight to her, and she says, "Thank you for a very lovely evening."

I didn't feel quite so terrific.

When I said goodnight to the third girl I took out, she's got her mouth open, ready to speak, and I say, "Thank you for a very lovely evening!"

She says, "Thank you—uh—Oh!—Yes—uh, I had a lovely evening, too, thank you!"

One time I was at a party with my beach crowd, and one of the older guys was in the kitchen teaching us how to kiss, using his girlfriend to demonstrate: "You have to have your lips like this, at right angles, so the noses don't collide," and so on. So I go into the living room and find a girl. I'm sitting on the couch with my arm around her, practicing this new art, when suddenly there's all kinds of excitement: "Arlene is coming! Arlene is coming!" I don't know who Arlene is.

Then someone says, "She's here! She's here!"—and everybody stops what they're doing and jumps up to see this queen. Arlene was very pretty, and I could see why she had all this admiration—it was well deserved—but I didn't believe in this undemocratic business of changing what you're doing just because the queen is coming in.

So, while everybody's going over to see Arlene, I'm still sitting there on the couch with my girl.

(Arlene told me later, after I had gotten to know her, that she remembered that party with all the nice people—except for one guy who was over in the corner on the couch smooching with a girl. What she didn't know was that two minutes before, all the others were doin' it too!)

The first time I ever said anything to Arlene was at a dance. She was very popular, and everybody was cutting in and dancing with her. I remember thinking I'd like to dance with her, too, and trying to decide when to cut in. I always had trouble with that problem: first of all, when she's over on the other side of the dance floor dancing with some guy, it's too complicated—so you wait until they come closer. Then when she's near you, you think, "Well, no, this isn't the kind of music I'm good at dancing to." So you wait for another type of music. When the music changes to something you like, you sort of step forward—at least you *think* you step forward to cut in—when some other guy cuts in just in front of you. So now you have to wait a few minutes because it's impolite to cut in too soon after someone else has. And by the time a few minutes have passed, they're over at the other side of the dance floor again, or the music has changed again, or whatever!

After a certain amount of this stalling and fooling around, I finally mutter something about wanting to dance with Arlene. One of the guys I was hanging around with overhears me and makes a big announcement to the other guys: "Hey, listen to this, guys; Feynman wants to dance with Arlene!" Soon one of them is dancing with Arlene and they dance over towards the rest of us. The others push me out onto the dance floor and I finally "cut in." You can see the condition I was in by my first words to her, which were an honest question: "How does it feel to be so popular?" We only danced a few minutes before somebody else cut in.

My friends and I had taken dancing lessons, although none of us would ever admit it. In those Depression days, a friend of my mother was trying to make a living by teaching dancing in the evening, in an upstairs dance studio. There was a back door to the place, and she arranged it so the young men could come up through the back way without being seen.

Every once in a while there would be a social dance at this

lady's studio. I didn't have the nerve to test this analysis, but it seemed to me that the girls had a much harder time than the boys did. In those days, girls couldn't ask to cut in and dance with boys; it wasn't "proper." So the girls who weren't very pretty would sit for hours at the side, just sad as hell.

I thought, "The guys have it easy: they're free to cut in whenever they want." But it wasn't easy. You're "free," but you haven't got the guts, or the sense, or whatever it takes to relax and enjoy dancing. Instead, you tie yourself in knots worrying about cutting in or inviting a girl to dance with you.

For example, if you saw a girl who was not dancing, who you thought you'd like to dance with, you might think, "Good! Now at least I've got a chance!" But it was usually very difficult: often the girl would say, "No, thank you, I'm tired. I think I'll sit this one out." So you go away somewhat defeated—but not completely, because maybe she really *is* tired—when you turn around and some other guy comes up to her, and there she is, dancing with him! Maybe this guy is her boyfriend and she knew he was coming over, or maybe she didn't like the way you look, or maybe something else. It was always so complicated for such a simple matter.

One time I decided to invite Arlene to one of these dances. It was the first time I took her out. My best friends were also at the dance; my mother had invited them, to get more customers for her friend's dance studio. These guys were contemporaries of mine, guys my own age from school. Harold Gast and David Leff were literary types, while Robert Stapler was a scientific type. We would spend a lot of time together after school, going on walks and discussing this and that.

Anyway, my best friends were at the dance, and as soon as they saw me with Arlene, they called me into the cloakroom and said, "Now listen, Feynman, we want you to understand that *we* understand that Arlene is *your* girl tonight, and we're not gonna bother you with her. She's out of bounds for us," and so on. But before long, there was cutting in and competition coming from precisely these guys! I learned the meaning of Shakespeare's phrase "Methinks thou dost protest too much."

You must appreciate what I was like then. I was a very shy character, always feeling uncomfortable because everybody was stronger than I, and always afraid I would look like a sissy. Everybody else played baseball; everybody else did all kinds of athletic things. If there was a game somewhere, and a ball would come rolling across the road, I would be petrified that maybe I'd have to pick it up and throw it back—because if I threw it, it would be about a radian off the correct direction, and not anywhere near the distance! And then everybody would laugh. It was terrible, and I was very unhappy about it.

One time I was invited to a party at Arlene's house. Everybody was there because Arlene was the most popular girl around: she was number one, the nicest girl, and everybody liked her. Well, I'm sitting in a big armchair with nothing to do, when Arlene comes over and sits on the arm of the chair to talk to me. That was the beginning of the feeling, "Oh, boy! The world is just wonderful now! Somebody I like has paid attention to me!"

In those days, in Far Rockaway, there was a youth center for Jewish kids at the temple. It was a big club that had many activities. There was a writers group that wrote stories and would read them to each other; there was a drama group that put on plays; there was a science group, and an art group. I had no interest in any subject except science, but Arlene was in the art group, so I joined it too. I struggled with the art business—learning how to make plaster casts of the face and so on (which I used much later in life, it turned out)—just so I could be in the same group with Arlene.

But Arlene had a boyfriend named Jerome in the group, so there was no chance for me. I just hovered around in the background.

One time, when I wasn't there, somebody nominated me for president of the youth center. The elders began getting nervous, because I was an avowed atheist by that time.

I had been brought up in the Jewish religion—my family went to the temple every Friday, I was sent to what we called "Sunday school," and I even studied Hebrew for a while—but at the same time, my father was telling me about the world. When I would hear the rabbi tell about some miracle such as a bush whose leaves were shaking but there wasn't any wind, I would try to fit the miracle into the real world and explain it in terms of natural phenomena.

Some miracles were harder than others to understand. The one about the leaves was easy. When I was walking to school, I heard a little noise: although the wind was hardly noticeable, the leaves of a bush were wiggling a little bit because they were in just the right position to make a kind of resonance. And I thought, "Aha! This is a good explanation for Elijah's vision of the quaking bush!"

But there were some miracles I never did figure out. For instance, there was a story in which Moses throws down his staff and it turns into a snake. I couldn't figure out what the witnesses saw that made them think his staff was a snake.

If I had thought back to when I was much younger, the Santa

Claus story could have provided a clue for me. But it didn't hit me hard enough at the time to produce the possibility that I should doubt the truth of stories that don't fit with nature. When I found out that Santa Claus wasn't real, I wasn't upset; rather, I was relieved that there was a much simpler phenomenon to explain how so many children all over the world got presents on the same night! The story had been getting pretty complicated—it was getting out of hand.

Santa Claus was a particular custom we celebrated in our family, and it wasn't very serious. But the miracles I was hearing about were connected with real things: there was the temple, where people would go every week; there was the Sunday school, where rabbis taught children about miracles; it was much more of a dramatic thing. Santa Claus didn't involve big institutions like the temple, which I knew were real.

So all the time I was going to the Sunday school, I was believing everything and having trouble putting it together. But of course, ultimately, it had to come to a crisis, sooner or later.

The actual crisis came when I was eleven or twelve. The rabbi was telling us a story about the Spanish Inquisition, in which the Jews suffered terrible tortures. He told us about a particular individual whose name was Ruth, exactly what she was supposed to have done, what the arguments were in her favor and against her—the whole thing, as if it had all been documented by a court reporter. And I was just an innocent kid, listening to all this stuff and believing it was a true commentary, because the rabbi had never indicated otherwise.

At the end, the rabbi described how Ruth was dying in prison: "And she thought, while she was dying"—blah, blah.

That was a shock to me. After the lesson was over, I went up to him and said, "How did they know what she thought when she was dying?"

He says, "Well, of course, in order to explain more vividly how the Jews suffered, we made up the story of Ruth. It wasn't a real individual."

That was too much for me. I felt terribly deceived: I wanted the straight story—not fixed up by somebody else—so I could decide for myself what it meant. But it was difficult for me to argue with adults. All I could do was get tears in my eyes. I started to cry, I was so upset.

He said, "What's the matter?"

I tried to explain. "I've been listening to all these stories, and now I don't know, of all the things you told me, which were true, and which were not true! I don't know what to do with everything that I've learned!" I was trying to explain that I was losing everything at the moment, because I was no longer sure of the data, so to speak. Here I had been struggling to understand all these miracles, and now—well, it solved a lot of miracles, all right! But I was unhappy.

The rabbi said, "If it is so traumatic for you, why do you come to Sunday school?"

"Because my parents make me."

I never talked to my parents about it, and I never found out whether the rabbi communicated with them or not, but my parents never made me go again. And it was just before I was supposed to get confirmed as a believer.

Anyway, that crisis resolved my difficulty rather rapidly, in favor of the theory that all the miracles were stories made up to help people understand things "more vividly," even if they conflicted with natural phenomena. But I thought nature itself was so interesting that I didn't want it distorted like that. And so I gradually came to disbelieve the whole religion.

Anyway, the Jewish elders had organized this club with all its activities not just to get us kids off the street, but to get us interested in the Jewish way of life. So to have someone like me elected as president would have made them very embarrassed. To our mutual relief I wasn't elected, but the center eventually failed anyway—it was on its way out when I was nominated, and had I been elected, I surely would have been blamed for its demise.

One day Arlene told me Jerome isn't her boyfriend anymore. She's not tied up with him. That was a big excitement for me, the beginning of *hope!* She invited me over to her house, at 154 Westminster Avenue in nearby Cedarhurst.

When I went to her house that time, it was dark and the porch wasn't lit. I couldn't see the numbers. Not wanting to disturb anyone by asking if it was the right house, I crawled up, quietly, and felt the numbers on the door: 154.

Arlene was having trouble with her homework in philosophy class. "We're studying Descartes," she said. "He starts out with 'Cogito, ergo sum'—'I think, therefore I am'—and ends up proving the existence of God."

"Impossible!" I said, without stopping to think that I was doubting the great Descartes. (It was a reaction I learned from my father: have no respect *whatsoever* for authority; forget who said it and instead look at what he starts with, where he ends up, and ask yourself, "Is it reasonable?") I said, "How can you deduce one from the other?"

"I don't know," she said.

"Well, let's look it over," I said. "What's the argument?"

So we look it over, and we see that Descartes' statement "Cogito, ergo sum" is supposed to mean that there is one thing that cannot be doubted—doubt itself. "Why doesn't he just say it straight?" I complained. "He just means somehow or other that he has one fact that he knows."

Then it goes on and says things like, "I can only imagine imperfect thoughts, but imperfect can only be understood as referent to the perfect. Hence the perfect must exist somewhere." (He's workin' his way towards God now.)

"Not at all!" I say. "In science you can talk about relative degrees of approximation without having a perfect theory. I don't know what this is all about. I think it's a bunch of baloney."

Arlene understood me. She understood, when she looked at it, that no matter how impressive and important this philosophy stuff was supposed to be, it could be taken lightly—you could just think about the words, instead of worrying about the fact that Descartes said it. "Well, I guess it's okay to take the other side," she said. "My teacher keeps telling us, 'There are two sides to every question, just like there are two sides to every piece of paper.'"

"There's two sides to that, too," I said.

"What do you mean?"

I had read about the Möbius strip in the *Britannica*, my wonderful *Britannica!* In those days, things like the Möbius strip weren't so well known to everybody, but they were just as understandable as they are to kids today. The existence of such a surface was so real: it wasn't a wishy-washy political question, or anything that you needed history to understand. Reading about those things was like being way off in a wonderful world that nobody knows about, and you're getting a kick not only from the delight of learning the stuff itself, but also from making yourself unique.

I got a strip of paper, put a half twist in it, and made it into a loop. Arlene was delighted.

The next day, in class, she lay in wait for her teacher. Sure enough, he holds up a piece of paper and says, "There are two sides to every question, just like there are two sides to every piece of paper." Arlene holds up her own strip of paper—with a half twist in it—and says, "Sir, there are even two sides to *that* question: there's paper with only one side!" The teacher and the class got all excited, and Arlene got such a kick out of showing them the Möbius strip that I think she paid more attention to me after that on account of it.

But after Jerome, I had a new competitor—my "good friend" Harold Gast. Arlene was always making up her mind one way or the other. When it came time for graduation, she went with Harold to the senior prom, but sat with my parents for the graduation ceremony.

I was the best in science, the best in mathematics, the best in physics, and the best in chemistry, so I was going up to the stage and receiving honors many times at the ceremony. Harold was the best in English and the best in history, and had written the school play, so that was very impressive.

I was terrible in English. I couldn't stand the subject. It seemed to me ridiculous to worry about whether you spelled something wrong or not, because English spelling is just a human convention—it has nothing to do with anything *real*, anything from nature. Any word can be spelled just as well a different way. I was impatient with all this English stuff.

There was a series of exams called the Regents, which the State of New York gave to every high school student. A few months before, when we all were taking the Regents examination in English, Harold and the other literary friend of mine, David Leff—the editor of the school newspaper—asked me which books I had chosen to write about. David had chosen something with profound social implications by Sinclair Lewis, and Harold had picked some playwright. I said I chose *Treasure Island* because we had that book in first-year English, and told them what I wrote.

They laughed. "Boy, are *you* gonna flunk, saying such simple stuff about such a simple book!"

There was also a list of questions for an essay. The one I chose was "The Importance of Science in Aviation." I thought, "What a dumb question! The importance of science in aviation is obvious!"

I was about to write a simple theme about this dumb question when I remembered that my literary friends were always "throwing the bull"—building up their sentences to sound complex and sophisticated. I decided to try it, just for the hell of it. I thought, "If the Regents are so silly as to have a subject like the importance of science in aviation, I'm gonna *do* that."

So I wrote stuff like, "Aeronautical science is important in the analysis of the eddies, vortices, and whirlpools formed in the atmosphere behind the aircraft . . ."—I knew that eddies, vortices, and whirlpools are the same thing, but mentioning them three different ways *sounds* better! That was the only thing I would not have ordinarily done on the test.

The teacher who corrected my examination must have been impressed by eddies, vortices, and whirlpools, because I got a 91 on the exam—while my literary friends, who chose topics the English teachers could more easily take issue with, both got 88.

That year a new rule came out: if you got 90 or better on a Regents examination, you automatically got honors in that subject at graduation! So while the playwright and the editor of the school newspaper had to stay in their seats, this illiterate fool physics student was called to go up to the stage once again and receive honors in English!

After the graduation ceremony, Arlene was in the hall with my parents and Harold's parents when the head of the math department came over. He was a very strong man—he was also the school disciplinarian—a tall, dominating fellow. Mrs. Gast says to him, "Hello, Dr. Augsberry. I'm Harold Gast's mother. And this is Mrs. Feynman . . ."

He completely ignores Mrs. Gast and immediately turns to my mother. "Mrs. Feynman, I want to impress upon you that a young man like your son comes along only very rarely. The state should support a man of such talent. You must be *sure* that he goes to college, the best college you can afford!" He was concerned that my parents might not be planning to send me to college, for in those days lots of kids had to get a job immediately after graduation to help support the family.

That in fact happened to my friend Robert. He had a lab, too, and taught me all about lenses and optics. (One day he had an accident in his lab. He was opening carbolic acid and the bottle jerked, spilling some acid on his face. He went to the doctor and had bandages put on for a few weeks. The funny thing was, when they took the bandages off his skin was smooth underneath, nicer than it had been before—there were many fewer blemishes. I've since found out that there was, for a while, some kind of a beauty treatment using carbolic acid in a more dilute form.) Robert's mother was poor, and he had to go to work right away to support her, so he couldn't continue his interest in the sciences.

Anyway, my mother reassured Dr. Augsberry: "We're saving money as best we can, and we're trying to send him to Columbia or MIT." And Arlene was listening to all this, so after that I was a little bit ahead.

Arlene was a wonderful girl. She was the editor of the newspaper at Nassau County Lawrence High School; she played the piano beautifully, and was very artistic. She made some decorations for our house, like the parrot on the inside of our closet. As time went on, and our family got to know her better, she would go to the woods to paint with my father, who had taken up painting in later life, as many people do.

Arlene and I began to mold each other's personality. She lived in a family that was very polite, and was very sensitive to other people's feelings. She taught me to be more sensitive to those kinds of things, too. On the other hand, her family felt that "white lies" were okay.

I thought one should have the attitude of "What do *you* care what other people think!" I said, "We should listen to other people's opinions and take them into account. Then, if they don't make sense and we think they're wrong, then that's that!"

Arlene caught on to the idea right away. It was easy to talk her into thinking that in our relationship, we must be very honest with each other and say everything straight, with absolute frankness. It worked very well, and we became very much in love—a love like no other love that I know of.

After that summer I went away to college at MIT. (I couldn't go to Columbia because of the Jewish quota.*) I began getting letters from my friends that said things like, "You should see how Arlene is going out with Harold," or "She's doing this and she's doing that, while you're all alone up there in Boston." Well, I was taking out girls in Boston, but they didn't mean a thing to me, and I knew the same was true with Arlene.

When summer came, I stayed in Boston for a summer job, and worked on measuring friction. The Chrysler Company had developed a new method of polishing to get a super finish, and we were supposed to measure how much better it was. (It turned out that the "super finish" was not significantly better.)

Anyway, Arlene found a way to be near me. She found a summer job in Scituate, about twenty miles away, taking care of children. But my father was concerned that I would become too involved with Arlene and get off the track of my studies, so he talked her out of it—or talked me out of it (I can't remember). Those days were very, very different from now. In those days, you had to go all the way up in your career before marrying.

I was able to see Arlene only a few times that summer, but we promised each other we would marry after I finished school. I had known her for six years by that time. I'm a little tongue-tied trying to describe to you how much our love for each other developed, but we were sure we were right for each other.

After I graduated from MIT I went to Princeton, and I would go home on vacations to see Arlene. One time when I went

---

* The quota system was a discriminatory practice of limiting the number of places in a university available to students of Jewish background.

to see her, Arlene had developed a bump on one side of her neck. She was a very beautiful girl, so it worried her a little bit, but it didn't hurt, so she figured it wasn't too serious. She went to her uncle, who was a doctor. He told her to rub it with omega oil.

Then, sometime later, the bump began to change. It got bigger—or maybe it was smaller—and she got a fever. The fever got worse, so the family doctor decided Arlene should go to the hospital. She was told she had typhoid fever. Right away, as I still do today, I looked up the disease in medical books and read all about it.

When I went to see Arlene in the hospital, she was in quarantine—we had to put on special gowns when we entered her room, and so on. The doctor was there, so I asked him how the Wydell test came out—it was an absolute test for typhoid fever that involved checking for bacteria in the feces. He said, "It was negative."

"What? How can that be!" I said. "Why all these gowns, when you can't even find the bacteria in an experiment? Maybe she doesn't have typhoid fever!"

The result of that was that the doctor talked to Arlene's parents, who told me not to interfere. "After all, he's the doctor. You're only her fiancé."

I've found out since that such people don't know what they're doing, and get insulted when you make some suggestion or criticism. I realize that now, but I wish I had been much stronger then and told her parents that the doctor was an idiot—which he was—and didn't know what he was doing. But as it was, her parents were in charge of it.

Anyway, after a little while, Arlene got better, apparently: the swelling went down and the fever went away. But after some weeks the swelling started again, and this time she went to another doctor. This guy feels under her armpits and in her groin, and so on, and notices there's swelling in those places, too. He says the problem is in her lymphatic glands, but he doesn't yet know what the specific disease is. He will consult with other doctors.

As soon as I hear about it I go down to the library at Princeton and look up lymphatic diseases, and find "Swelling of the Lymphatic Glands. (1) Tuberculosis of the lymphatic glands. This is very easy to diagnose . . ."—so I figure this isn't what Arlene has, because the doctors are having trouble trying to figure it out.

I start reading about some other diseases: lymphodenema, lymphodenoma, Hodgkin's disease, all kinds of other things; they're all cancers of one crazy form or another. The only difference between lymphodenema and lymphodenoma was, as far as I could make out by reading it very carefully, that if the patient dies, it's lymphodenoma; if the patient survives—at least for a while—then it's lymphodenema.

At any rate, I read through all the lymphatic diseases, and decided that the most likely possibility was that Arlene had an incurable disease. Then I half smiled to myself, thinking, "I bet everybody who reads through a medical book thinks they have a fatal disease." And yet, after reading everything very carefully, I couldn't find any other possibility. It was serious.

Then I went to the weekly tea at Palmer Hall, and found myself talking to the mathematicians just as I always did, even though I had just found out that Arlene probably had a fatal disease. It was very strange—like having two minds.

When I went to visit her, I told Arlene the joke about the people who don't know any medicine reading the medical book and always assuming they have a fatal disease. But I also told her I thought we were in great difficulty, and that the best I could figure out was that she had an incurable disease. We discussed the various diseases, and I told her what each one was like.

One of the diseases I told Arlene about was Hodgkin's disease. When she next saw her doctor, she asked him about it: "Could it be Hodgkin's disease?"

He said, "Well, yes, that's a possibility."

When she went to the county hospital, the doctor wrote the following diagnosis: "Hodgkin's disease—?" So I realized that the doctor didn't know any more than I did about this problem.

The county hospital gave Arlene all sorts of tests and X-ray treatments for this "Hodgkin's disease—?" and there were special meetings to discuss this peculiar case. I remember waiting for her outside, in the hall. When the meeting was over, the nurse wheeled her out in a wheelchair. All of a sudden a little guy comes running out of the meeting room and catches up with us. "Tell me," he says, out of breath, "do you spit up blood? Have you ever coughed up blood?"

The nurse says, "Go away! Go away! What kind of thing is that to ask of a patient!"—and brushes him away. Then she turned to us and said, "That man is a doctor from the neighborhood who comes to the meetings and is always making trouble. That's not the kind of thing to ask of a patient!"

I didn't catch on. The doctor was checking a certain possibility, and if I had been smart, I would have asked him what it was.

Finally, after a lot of discussion, a doctor at the hospital tells me they figure the most likely possibility is Hodgkin's disease. He says, "There will be some periods of improvement, and some periods in the hospital. It will be on and off, getting gradually worse. There's no way to reverse it entirely. It's fatal after a few years."

"I'm sorry to hear that," I say. "I'll tell her what you said."

"No, no!" says the doctor. "We don't want to upset the patient. We're going to tell her it's glandular fever."

"No, no!" I reply. "We've already discussed the possibility of Hodgkin's disease. I know she can adjust to it."

"Her parents don't want her to know. You had better talk to them first."

At home, everybody worked on me: my parents, my two aunts, our family doctor; they were all on me, saying I'm a very foolish young man who doesn't realize what pain he's going to bring to this wonderful girl by telling her she has a fatal disease. "How can you do such a terrible thing?" they asked, in horror.

"Because we have made a pact that we must speak honestly with each other and look at everything directly. There's no use fooling around. She's gonna ask me what she's got, and I cannot lie to her!"

"Oh, that's childish!" they said—blah, blah, blah. Everybody kept working on me, and said I was wrong. I thought I was definitely right, because I had already talked to Arlene about the disease and knew she could face it—that telling her the truth was the right way to handle it.

But finally, my little sister comes up to me—she was eleven or twelve then—with tears running down her face. She beats me on the chest, telling me that Arlene is such a wonderful girl, and that I'm such a foolish, stubborn brother. I couldn't take it any more. That broke me down.

So I wrote Arlene a goodbye love letter, figuring that if she ever found out the truth after I had told her it was glandular fever, we would be through. I carried the letter with me all the time.

The gods never make it easy; they always make it harder. I go to the hospital to see Arlene—having made this decision—and there she is, sitting up in bed, surrounded by her parents, somewhat distraught. When she sees me, her face lights up and she says, "Now I know how valuable it is that we tell each other the truth!" Nodding at her parents, she continues, "They're telling me I have glandular fever, and I'm not sure whether I believe them or not. Tell me, Richard, do I have Hodgkin's disease or glandular fever?"

"You have glandular fever," I said, and I died inside. It was terrible—just terrible!

Her reaction was completely simple: "Oh! Fine! Then I believe them." Because we had built up so much trust in each other, she was completely relieved. Everything was solved, and all was very nice.

She got a little bit better, and went home for a while. About a week later, I get a telephone call. "Richard," she says, "I want to talk to you. Come on over."

"Okay." I made sure I still had the letter with me. I could tell something was the matter.

I go upstairs to her room, and she says, "Sit down." I sit down on the end of her bed. "All right, now tell me," she says, "do I have glandular fever or Hodgkin's disease?"

"You have Hodgkin's disease." And I reached for the letter.

"God!" she says. "They must have put you through hell!"

I had just told her she has a fatal disease, and was admitting that I had lied to her as well, and what does she think of? She's worried about *me!* I was terribly ashamed of myself. I gave Arlene the letter.

"You should have stuck by it. We know what we're doing; we are right!"

"I'm sorry. I feel awful."

"I understand, Richard. Just don't do it again."

You see, she was in bed upstairs, and did something she used to do when she was little: she tiptoed out of bed and crawled down the stairs a little bit to listen to what people were doing downstairs. She heard her mother crying a lot, and went back to bed thinking, "If I have glandular fever, why is Mother crying so much? But Richard said I had glandular fever, so it must be right!"

Later she thought, "Could *Richard* have lied to me?" and began to wonder how that might be possible. She concluded that, incredible as it sounded, somebody might have put me through a wringer of some sort.

She was so good at facing difficult situations that she went on to the next problem. "Okay," she says, "I have Hodgkin's disease. What are we going to do now?"

I had a scholarship at Princeton, and they wouldn't let me keep it if I got married. We knew what the disease was like: sometimes it would get better for some months, and Arlene could be at home, and then she would have to be in the hospital for some months—back and forth for two years, perhaps.

So I figure, although I'm in the middle of trying to get my Ph.D., I could get a job at the Bell Telephone Laboratories doing research—it was a very good place to work—and we could get a little apartment in Queens that wasn't too far from the hospital or Bell Labs. We could get married in a few months, in New York. We worked everything out that afternoon.

For some months now Arlene's doctors had wanted to take a biopsy of the swelling on her neck, but her parents didn't want it done—they didn't want to "bother the poor sick girl." But with new resolve, I kept working on them, explaining that it's important to get as much information as possible. With Arlene's help, I finally convinced her parents.

A few days later, Arlene telephones me and says, "They got a report from the biopsy."

"Yeah? Is it good or bad?"

"I don't know. Come over and let's talk about it."

When I got to her house, she showed me the report. It said, "Biopsy shows tuberculosis of the lymphatic gland."

That really got me. I mean, that was the first goddamn thing on the list! I passed it by, because the book said it was easy to diagnose, and because the doctors were having so much trouble trying to figure out what it was. I assumed they had checked the obvious case. And it *was* the obvious case: the man who had come running out of the meeting room asking "Do you spit up blood?" had the right idea. He knew what it probably was!

I felt like a jerk, because I had passed over the obvious possibility by using circumstantial evidence—which isn't any good—and by assuming the doctors were more intelligent than they were. Otherwise, I would have suggested it right off, and perhaps the doctor would have diagnosed Arlene's disease way back then as "tuberculosis of the lymphatic gland—?" I was a dope. I've learned, since then.

Anyway, Arlene says, "So I might live as long as seven years. I may even get better."

"So what do you mean, you don't know if it's good or bad?"

"Well, now we won't be able to get married until later."

Knowing that she only had two more years to live, we had solved things so perfectly, from her point of view, that she was disturbed to discover she'd live longer! But it didn't take me long to convince her it was a better circumstance.

So we knew we could face things together, from then on. After going through that, we had no difficulty facing any other problem.

When the war came, I was recruited to work on the Manhattan Project at Princeton, where I was finishing up my degree. A few months later, as soon as I got my degree, I announced to my family that I wanted to get married.

My father was horrified, because from the earliest times, as he saw me develop, he thought I would be happy as a scientist. He thought it was still too early to marry—it would interfere with my career. He also had this crazy idea: if a guy was in some difficulty, he used to always say, "Cherchez la femme"— look for the woman behind it. He felt that women were the great danger to a man, that a man always has to watch out and be tough about women. And when he sees me marrying a girl with tuberculosis, he thinks of the possibility that I'm going to get sick, too.

My whole family was worried about that—aunts, uncles, everyone. They brought the family doctor over to our house. He tried to explain to me that tuberculosis is a dangerous disease, and that I'm bound to get it.

I said, "Just tell me how it's transmitted, and we'll figure it out." We were already very, very careful: we knew we must not kiss, because there's a lot of bacteria in the mouth.

Then they very carefully explained to me that when I had promised to marry Arlene, I didn't know the situation. Everybody would understand that I didn't know the situation then, and that it didn't represent a real promise.

I never had that feeling, that crazy idea that they had, that I was getting married because I had promised it. I hadn't even *thought* of that. It wasn't a question of having promised anything; we had stalled around, not getting a piece of paper and not being formally married, but we were in love, and were already married, emotionally.

I said, "Would it be sensible for a husband who learns that his wife has tuberculosis to leave her?"

Only my aunt who ran the hotel thought maybe it would be all right for us to get married. Everybody else was still against it. But this time, since my family had given me this kind of advice before and it had been so wrong, I was in a much stronger position. It was very easy to resist and to just proceed. So there was no problem, really. Although it was a similar circumstance, they weren't going to convince me of anything any more. Arlene and I knew we were right in what we were doing.

Arlene and I worked everything out. There was a hospital in New Jersey just south of Fort Dix where she could stay while I was at Princeton. It was a charity hospital—Deborah was the name of it—supported by the Women's Garment Workers Union of New York. Arlene wasn't a garment worker, but it didn't make any difference. And I was just a young fella working on this project for the government, and the pay was very low. But this way I could take care of her, at last.

We decided to get married on the way to Deborah Hospital.

I went to Princeton to pick up a car—Bill Woodward, one of the graduate students there, lent me his station wagon. I fixed it up like a little ambulance, with a mattress and sheets in the back, so Arlene could lie down in case she got tired. Although this was one of the periods when the disease was apparently not so bad and she was at home, Arlene had been in the county hospital a lot, and she was a little weak.

I drove up to Cedarhurst and picked up my bride. Arlene's family waved goodbye, and off we went. We crossed Queens and Brooklyn, then went to Staten Island on the ferry—that was our romantic boat ride—and drove to the city hall for the Borough of Richmond to get married.

We went up the stairs, slowly, into the office. The guy there was very nice. He did everything right away. He said, "You don't have any witnesses," so he called the bookkeeper and an accountant from another room, and we were married according to the laws of the State of New York. Then we were very happy, and we smiled at each other, holding hands.

The bookkeeper says to me, "You're married now. You should kiss the bride!"

So the bashful character kissed his bride lightly on the cheek.

I gave everyone a tip and we thanked them very much. We got back in the car, and drove to Deborah Hospital.

Every weekend I'd go down from Princeton to visit Arlene. One time the bus was late, and I couldn't get into the hospital. There weren't any hotels nearby, but I had my old sheepskin coat on (so I was warm enough), and I looked for an empty lot to sleep in. I was a little worried what it might look like in the